# East

## Quiz Writing Journal

# QUIZ TIME

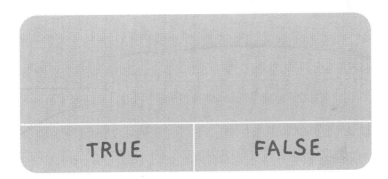

| | |
|---|---|
| TRUE | FALSE |

Quiz No:

A

B

C

D

Quiz No:

A

B

C

D

Quiz No:

A

B

C

D

Quiz No:

Quiz No:

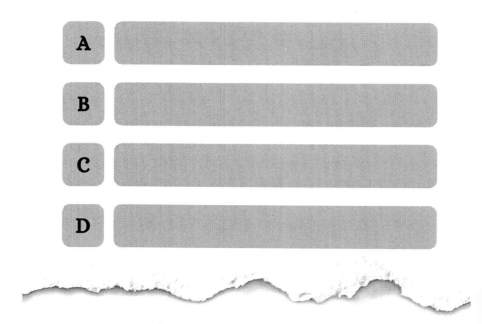

Quiz No:

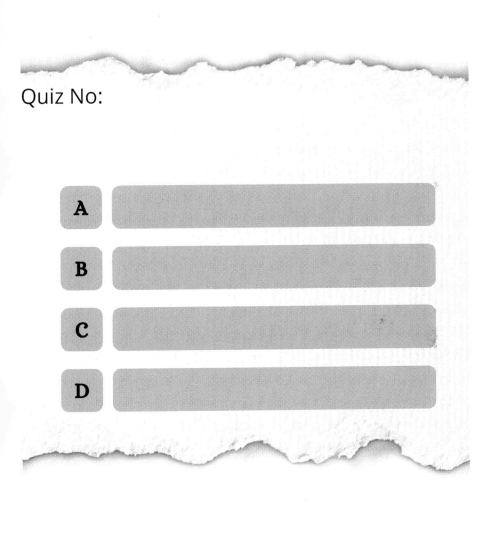

Quiz No:

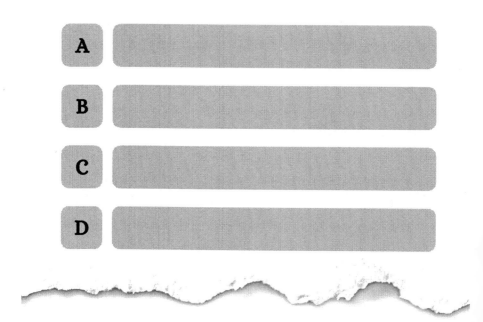

Quiz No:

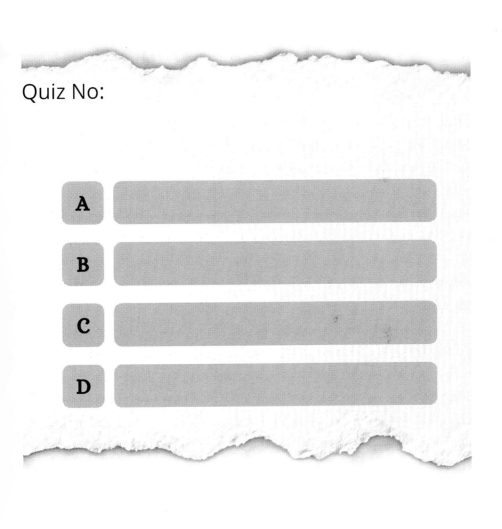

Quiz No:

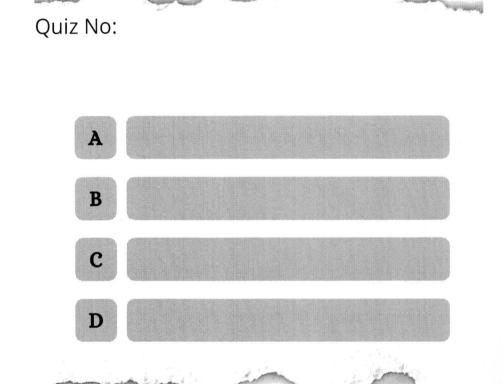

A

B

C

D

Quiz No:

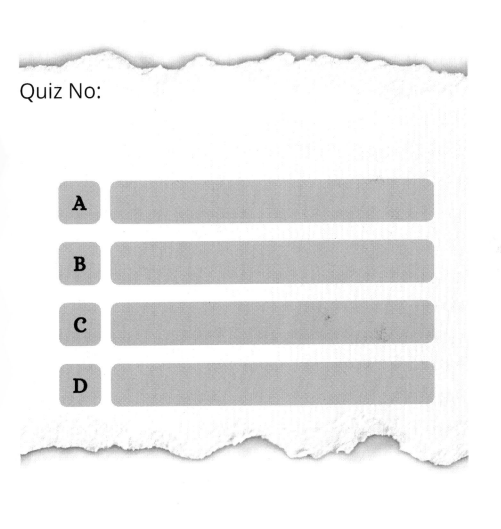

Quiz No:

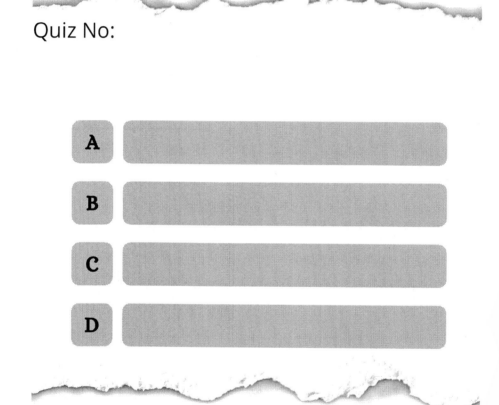

Quiz No:

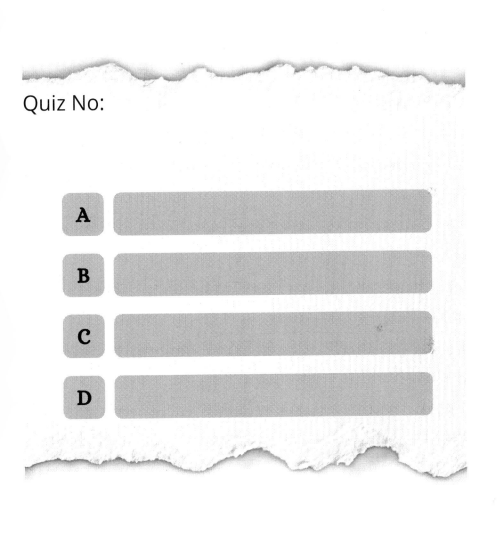

Quiz No:

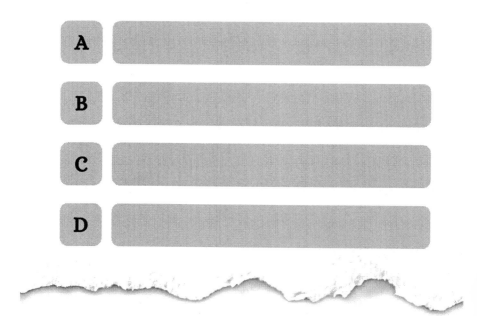

Quiz No:

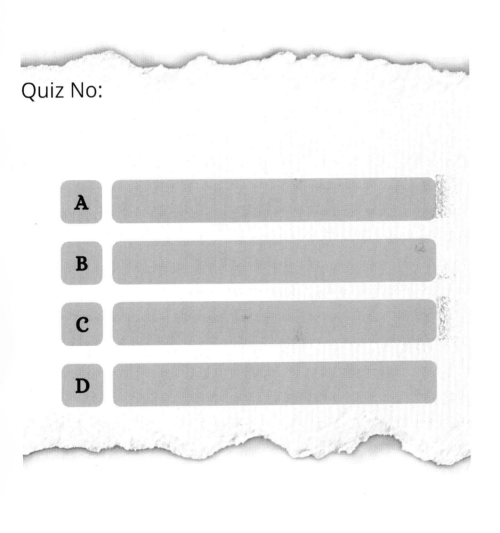

Quiz No:

Quiz No:

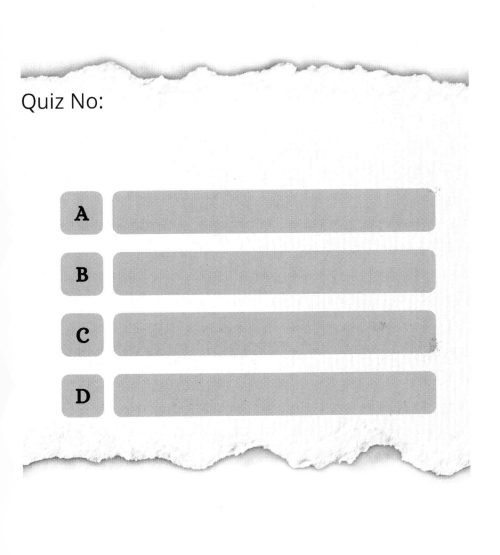

Quiz No:

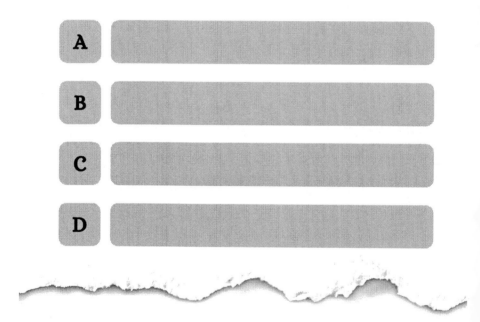

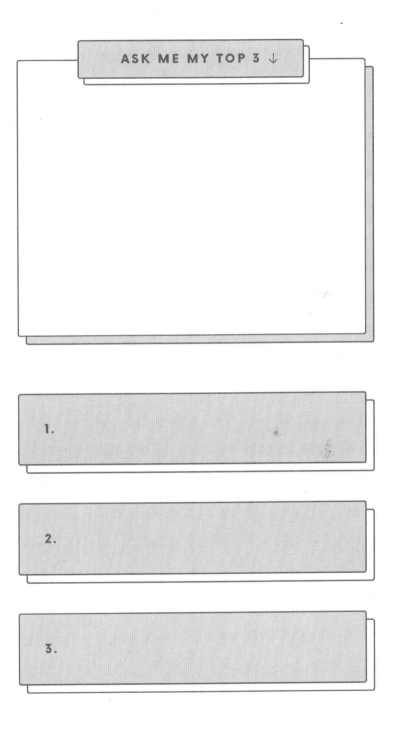

**ASK ME MY TOP 3 ↓**

1.

2.

3.

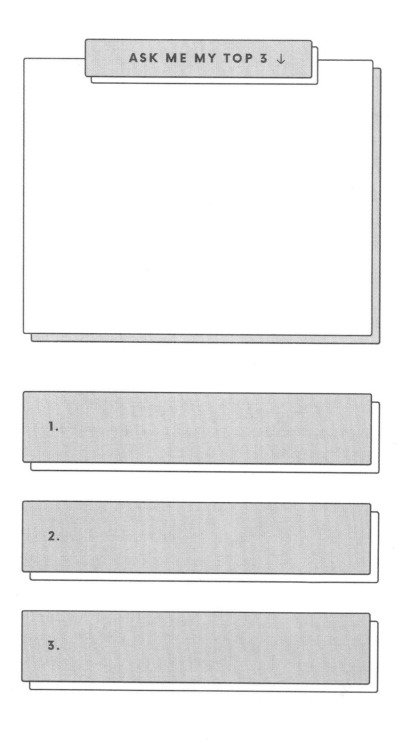

**ASK ME MY TOP 3** ↓

1.

2.

3.

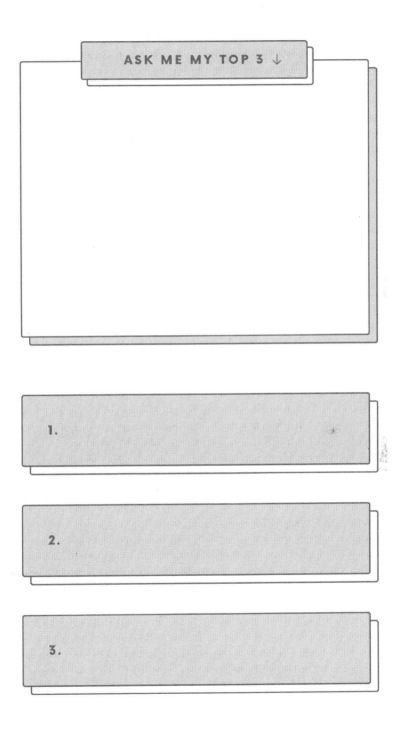

ASK ME MY TOP 3 ↓

1.

2.

3.

**ASK ME MY TOP 3** ↓

1.

2.

3.

**ASK ME MY TOP 3 ↓**

1.

2.

3.

## ASK ME MY TOP 3 ↓

1.

2.

3.

**ASK ME MY TOP 3 ↓**

1.

2.

3.

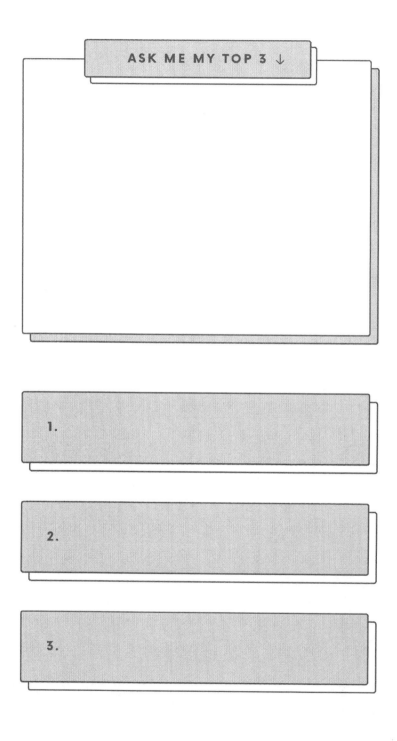

**ASK ME MY TOP 3** ↓

1.

2.

3.

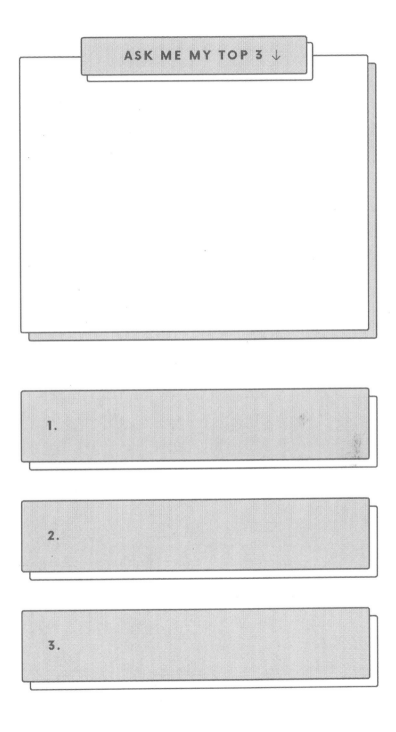

ASK ME MY TOP 3 ↓

1.

2.

3.

ASK ME MY TOP 3 ↓

1.

2.

3.

**ASK ME MY TOP 3** ↓

1.

2.

3.

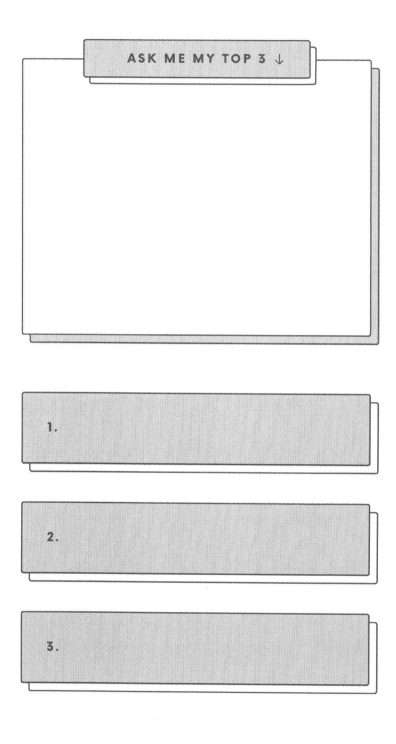

ASK ME MY TOP 3 ↓

1.

2.

3.

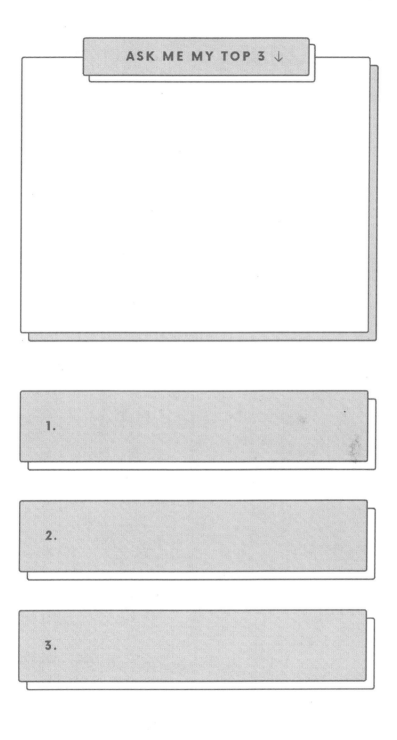

**ASK ME MY TOP 3 ↓**

1.

2.

3.

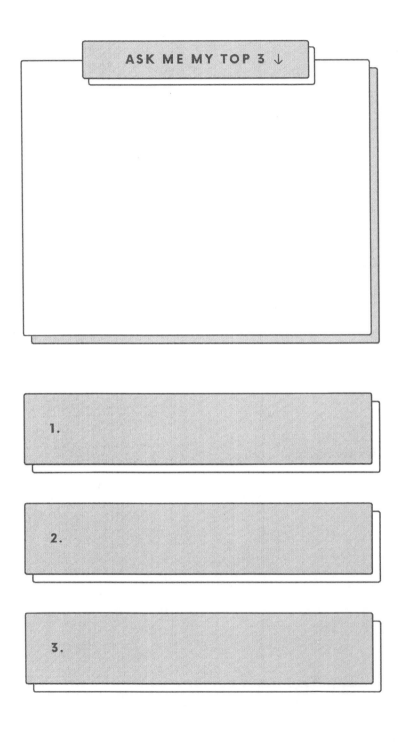

ASK ME MY TOP 3 ↓

1.

2.

3.

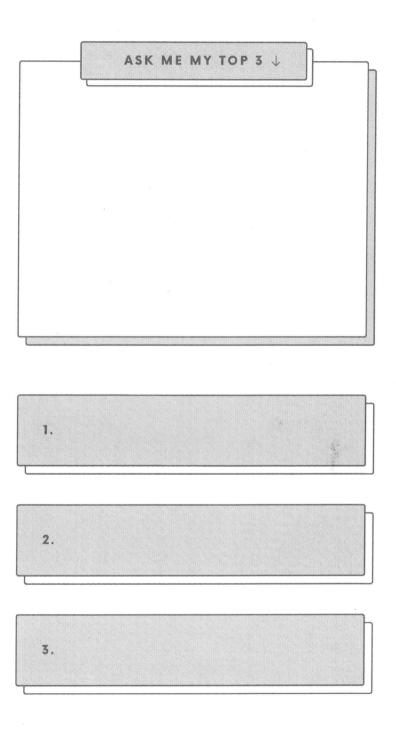

**ASK ME MY TOP 3** ↓

1.

2.

3.

ASK ME MY TOP 3 ↓

1.

2.

3.

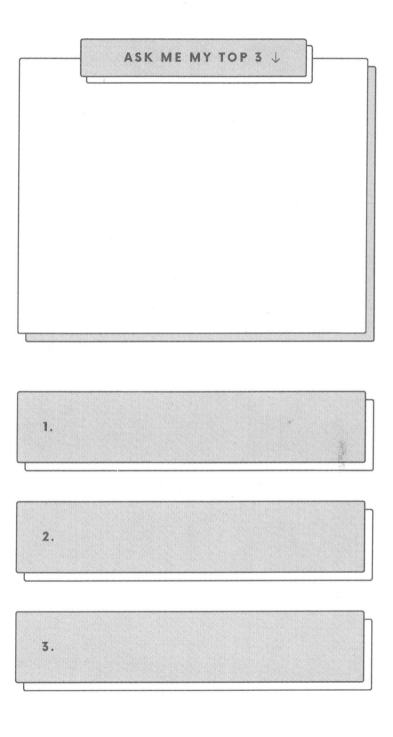

ASK ME MY TOP 3 ↓

1.

2.

3.

**ASK ME MY TOP 3 ↓**

1.

2.

3.

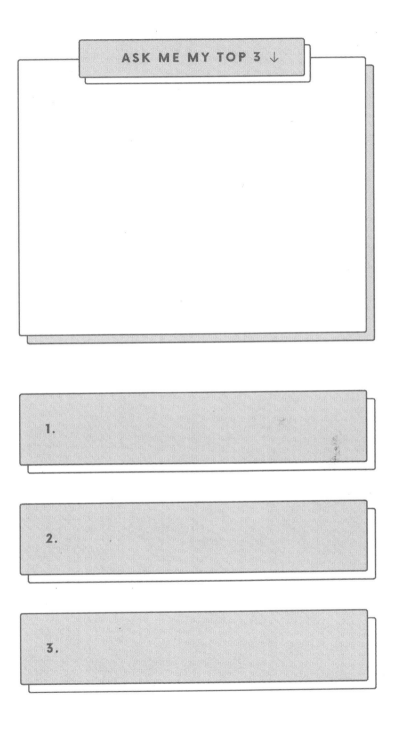

**ASK ME MY TOP 3 ↓**

1.

2.

3.

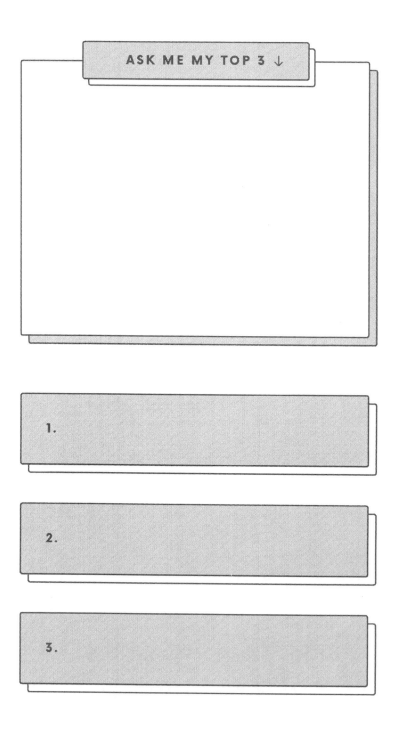

ASK ME MY TOP 3 ↓

1.

2.

3.

ASK ME MY TOP 3 ↓

1.

2.

3.

**ASK ME MY TOP 3 ↓**

1.

2.

3.

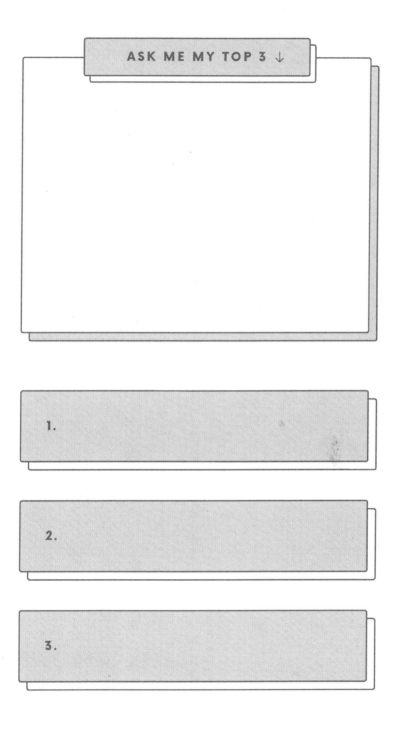

**ASK ME MY TOP 3 ↓**

1.

2.

3.

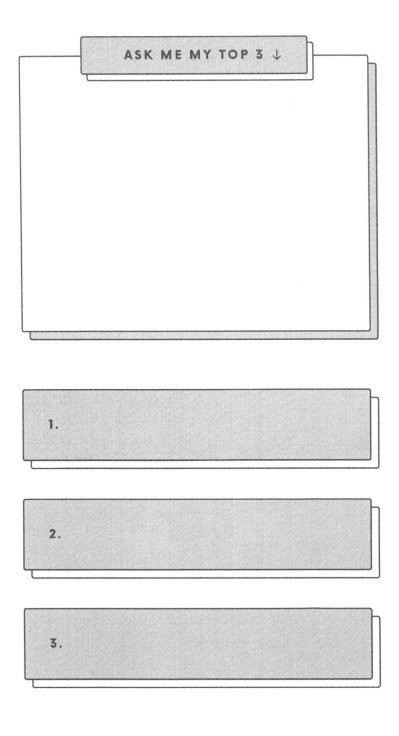

ASK ME MY TOP 3 ↓

1.

2.

3.

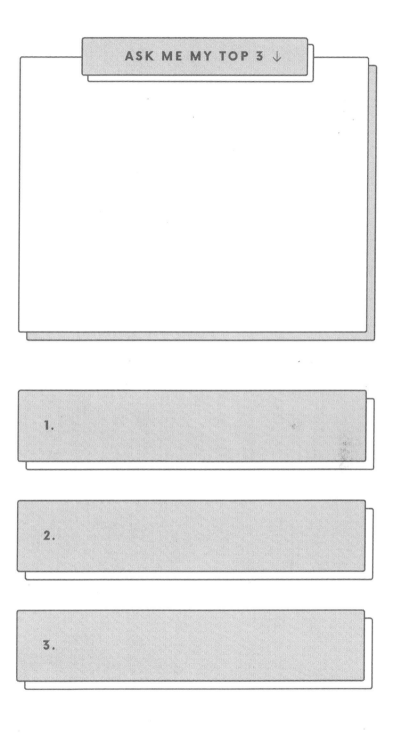

## ASK ME MY TOP 3 ↓

1.

2.

3.

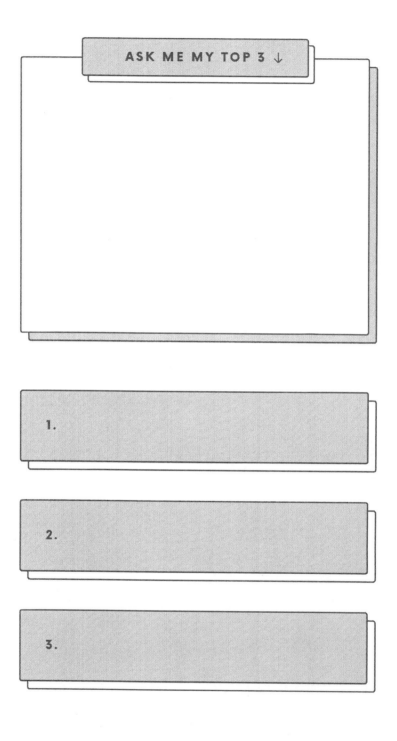

ASK ME MY TOP 3 ↓

1.

2.

3.

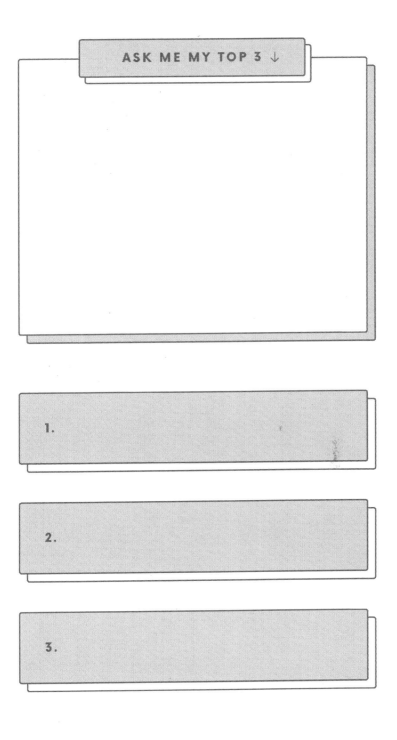

**ASK ME MY TOP 3 ↓**

1.

2.

3.

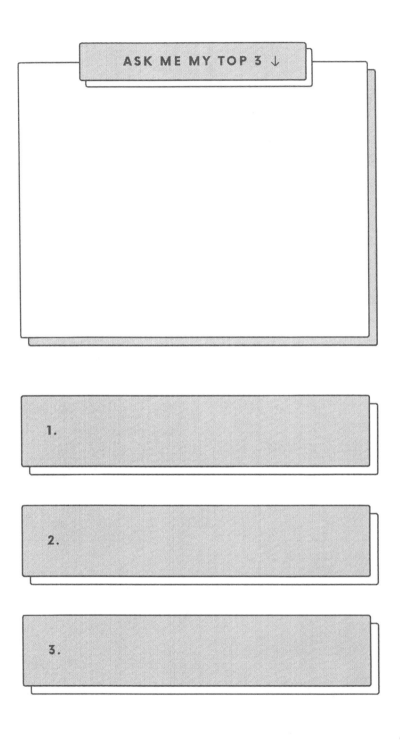

ASK ME MY TOP 3 ↓

1.

2.

3.

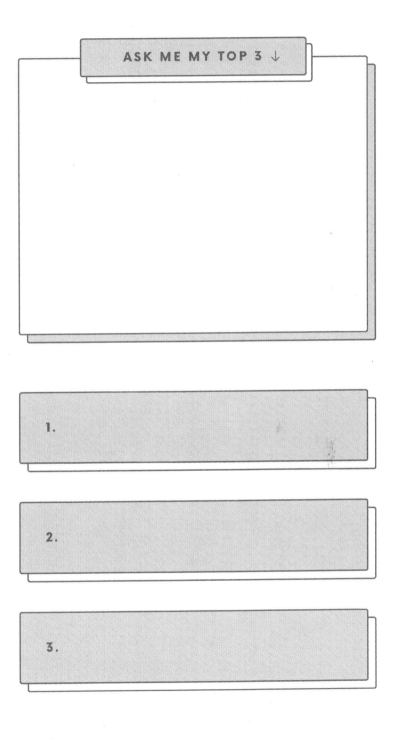

**ASK ME MY TOP 3 ↓**

1.

2.

3.

## ASK ME MY TOP 3 ↓

1.

2.

3.

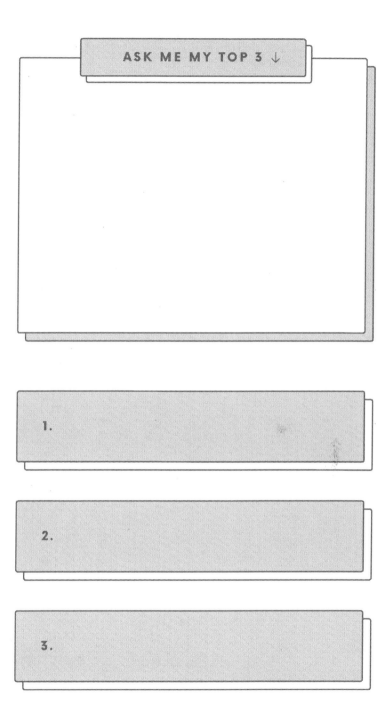

ASK ME MY TOP 3 ↓

1.

2.

3.

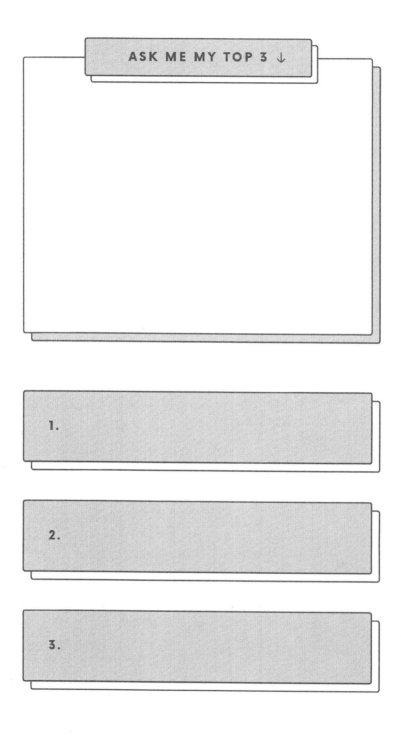

**ASK ME MY TOP 3** ↓

1.

2.

3.

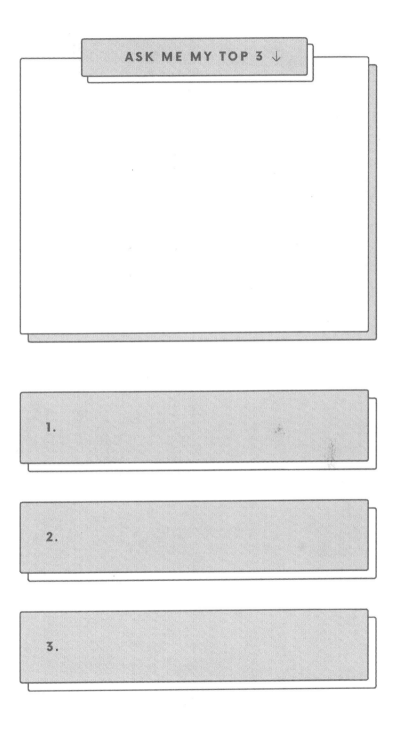

ASK ME MY TOP 3 ↓

1.

2.

3.

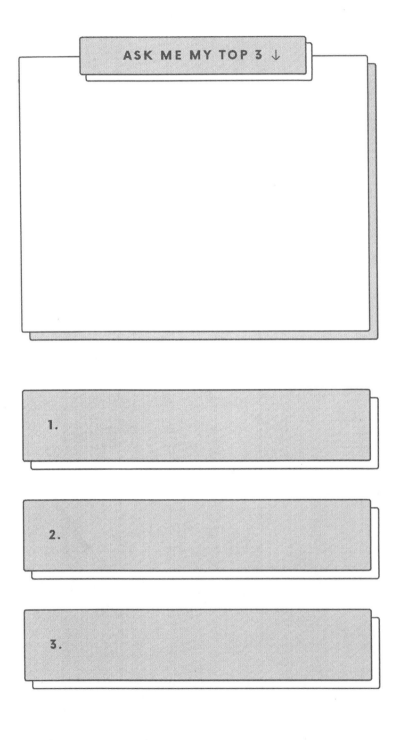

ASK ME MY TOP 3 ↓

1.

2.

3.

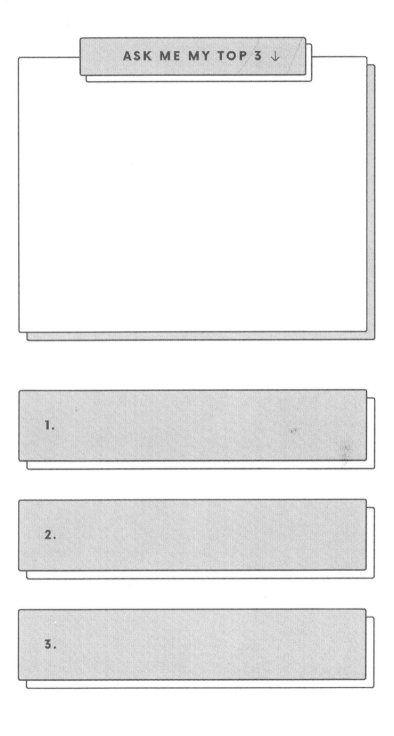

**ASK ME MY TOP 3 ↓**

1.

2.

3.

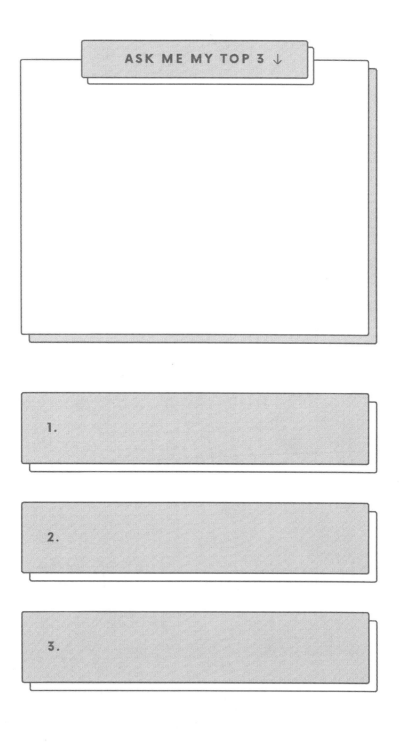

ASK ME MY TOP 3 ↓

1.

2.

3.

1.

2.

3.

ASK ME MY TOP 3 ↓

1.

2.

3.

## ASK ME MY TOP 3 ↓

1.

2.

3.

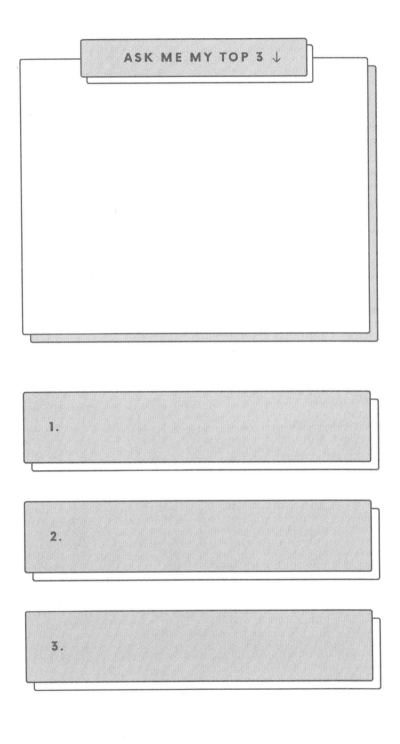

**ASK ME MY TOP 3 ↓**

1.

2.

3.

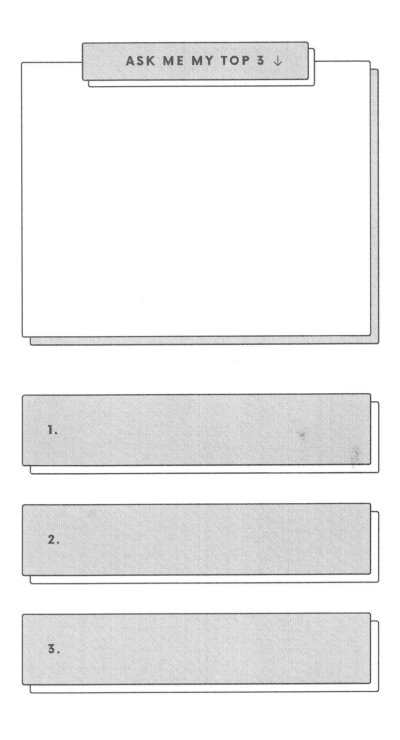

**ASK ME MY TOP 3** ↓

1.

2.

3.

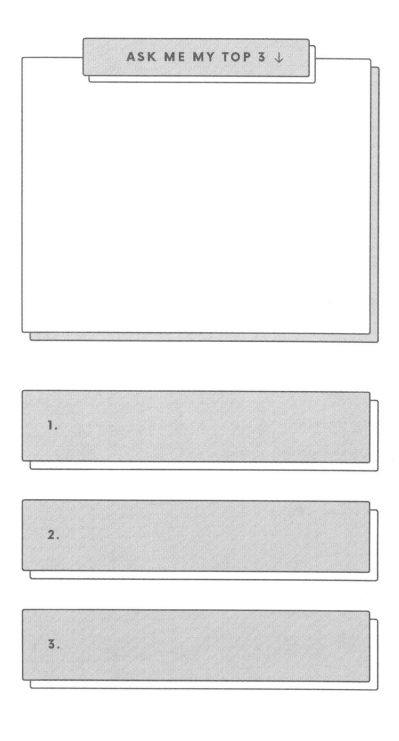

ASK ME MY TOP 3 ↓

1.

2.

3.

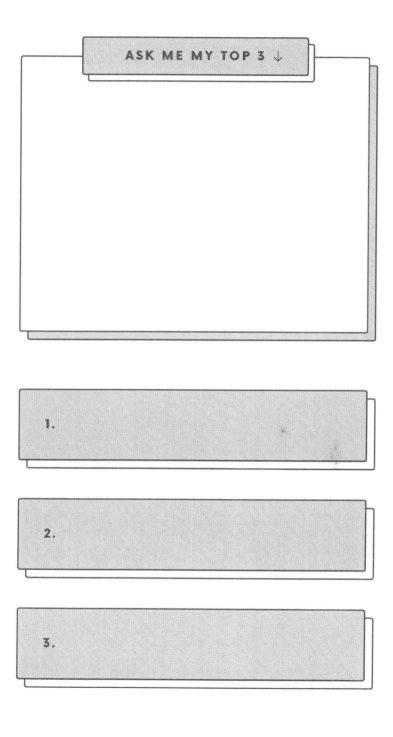

**ASK ME MY TOP 3 ↓**

1.

2.

3.

## ASK ME MY TOP 3 ↓

1.

2.

3.

## ASK ME MY TOP 3 ↓

1.

2.

3.

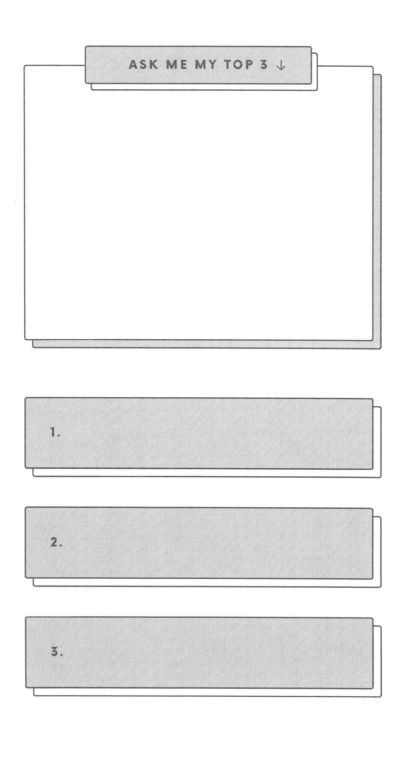

**ASK ME MY TOP 3** ↓

1.

2.

3.

## ASK ME MY TOP 3 ↓

**1.**

**2.**

**3.**

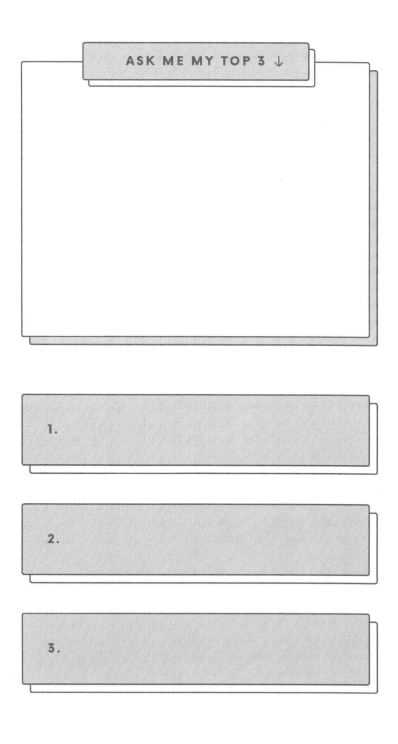

**ASK ME MY TOP 3 ↓**

1.

2.

3.

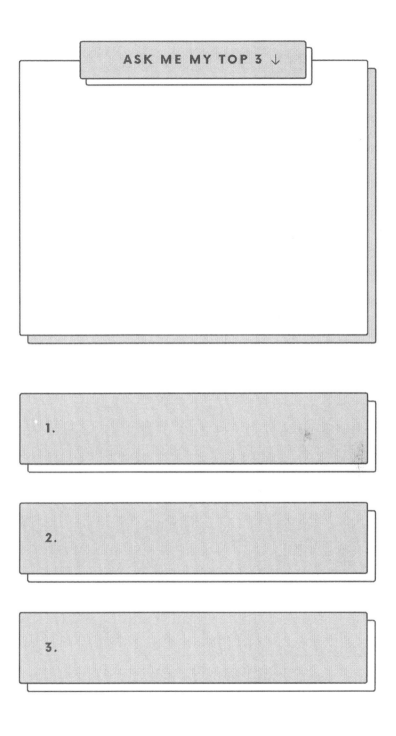

ASK ME MY TOP 3 ↓

1.

2.

3.

## ASK ME MY TOP 3 ↓

1.

2.

3.

## ASK ME MY TOP 3 ↓

1.

2.

3.

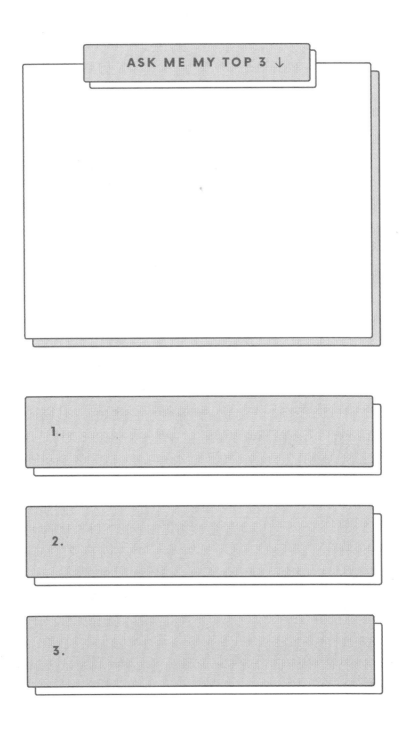

ASK ME MY TOP 3 ↓

1.

2.

3.

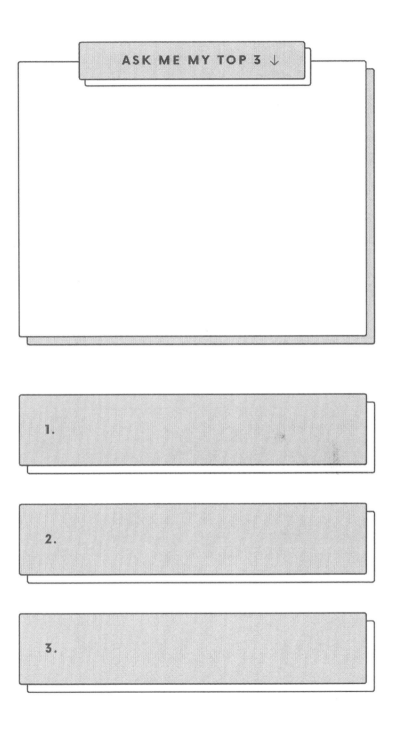

**ASK ME MY TOP 3 ↓**

1.

2.

3.

## ASK ME MY TOP 3 ↓

1.

2.

3.

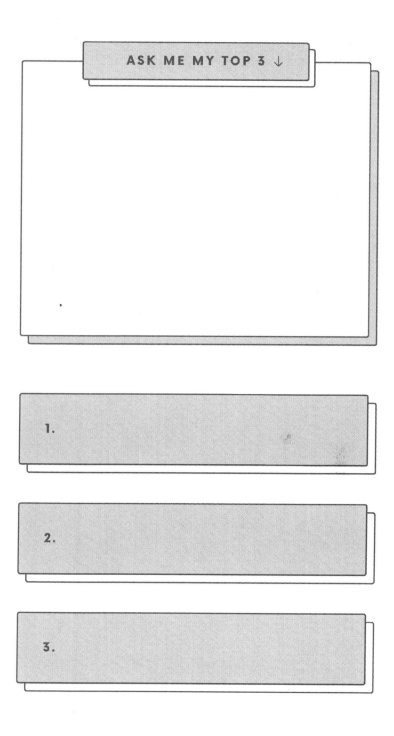

ASK ME MY TOP 3 ↓

1.

2.

3.

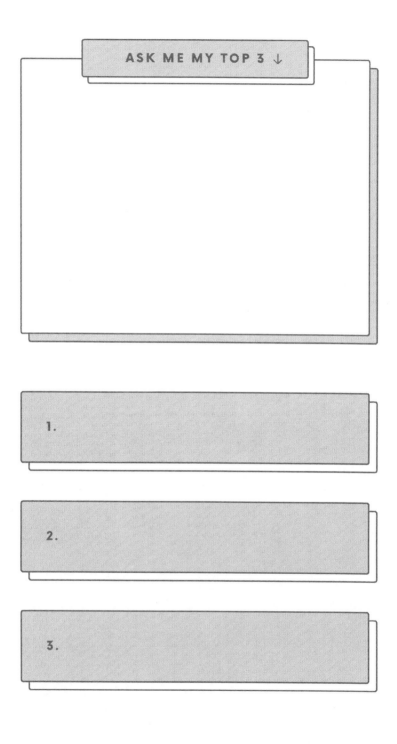

ASK ME MY TOP 3 ↓

1.

2.

3.

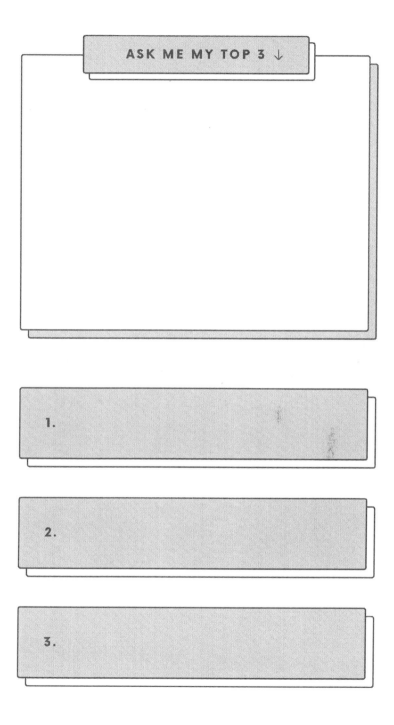

ASK ME MY TOP 3 ↓

1.

2.

3.

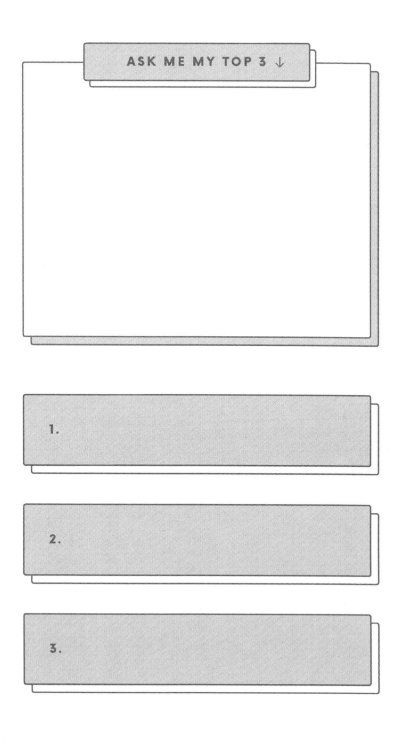

ASK ME MY TOP 3 ↓

1.

2.

3.

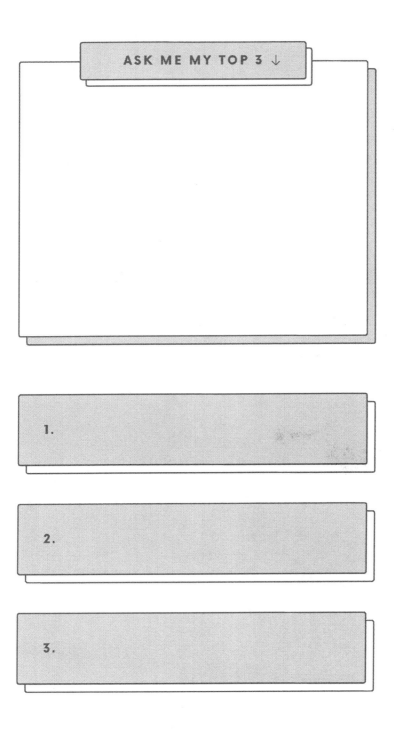

ASK ME MY TOP 3 ↓

1.

2.

3.

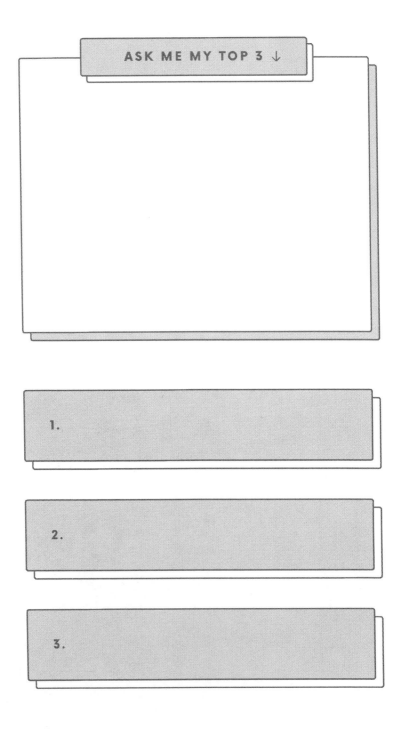

**ASK ME MY TOP 3 ↓**

1.

2.

3.

## ASK ME MY TOP 3 ↓

1.

2.

3.

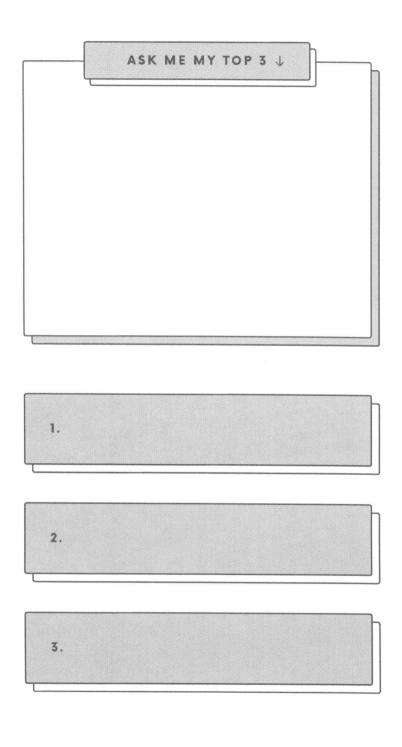

**ASK ME MY TOP 3** ↓

1.

2.

3.

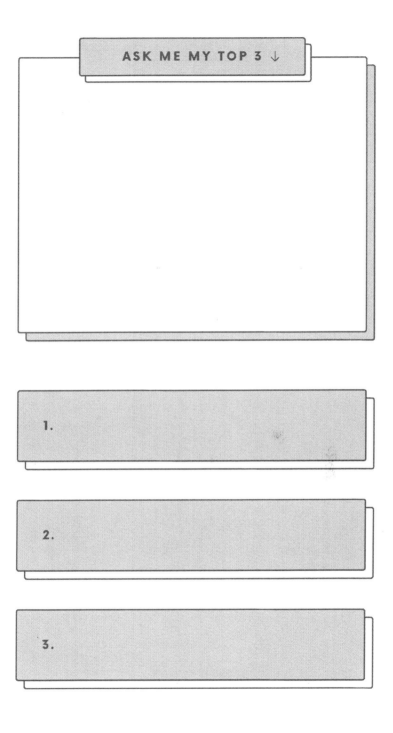

ASK ME MY TOP 3 ↓

1.

2.

3.

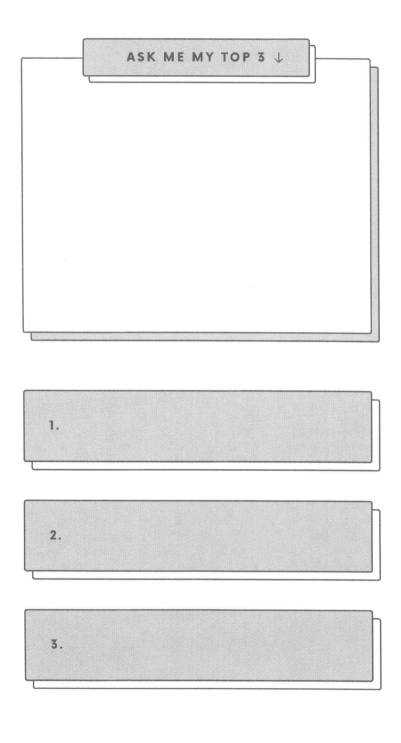

ASK ME MY TOP 3 ↓

1.

2.

3.

# Notes

# Notes

# Notes

# Notes

# Notes

# Notes

# Notes

# Notes

# Notes

# Notes

# Notes

# Notes

# Notes

# Notes

# Notes

# Notes

# Notes

# Notes

Made in the USA
Columbia, SC
20 November 2024

47133840R00057